The Animals of Alaska

John Rickus

Rosen REAL READERS

Rosen Classroom Books & Materials
New York

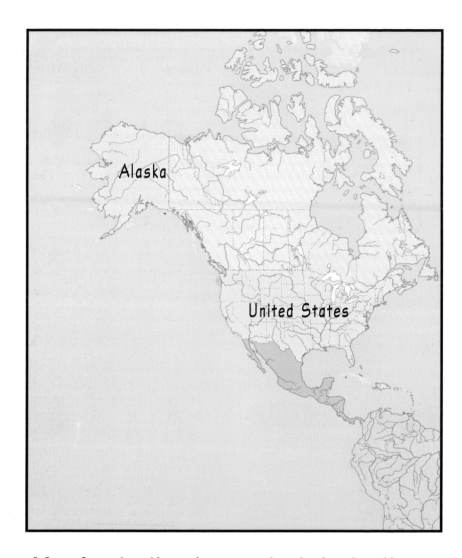

Alaska is the largest state in the United States. Many kinds of animals live in Alaska.

Alaska can be very cold because it is so far north. Animals in Alaska must have a way to keep warm.

A wolf has **thick** fur that keeps
it warm.

Reindeer have two coats of fur
that keep them warm.

Bears have thick fur that keeps them warm.

A **polar bear** lives where it
is always cold. A polar bear
has thick, white fur that keeps
it warm.

A moose has long legs that help
it walk in deep snow. A moose
also has fur to keep it warm.

An ox can have fur that almost reaches its feet! This keeps the ox warm and dry.

Some foxes have warm fur that is brown in the summer and white in the winter.

A walrus has thick fat to keep it warm!

Glossary

Alaska   One of the fifty states of the United States.

polar bear   A large, white bear that lives where it is always cold.

thick   Not thin.